CHAN — IES

Stories from Africa

These stories come from different countries in Africa. In Malawi, young Joey watches the great silver planes in the sky above him, and dreams of walking in the streets of London or Tokyo. But the longest journey he makes is to the airport rubbish dump, to meet his friend Mazambezi. In South Africa, life is not kind to Dadi-Ma. Where can she take her little grandson, to give him a better life? Her problems get worse and worse, but one thing does not change – her love for her grandson. And in Dar es Salaam it is an old, old, problem – children growing up and wanting to leave home, to go away, to cross the sea, to study . . . in a foreign country . . .

BOOKWORMS WORLD STORIES

English has become an international language, and is used on every continent, in many varieties, for all kinds of purposes. *Bookworms World Stories* are the latest addition to the Oxford Bookworms Library. Their aim is to bring the best of the world's stories to the English language learner, and to celebrate the use of English for storytelling all around the world.

Jennifer Bassett
Series Editor

They change their skies,
but not their souls,
who run across the sea.

Horace (65–8 BC), Epistles, I. xi. 27

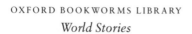

OXFORD BOOKWORMS LIBRARY
World Stories

Changing their Skies
Stories from Africa

Stage 2 (700 headwords)

Series Editor: Jennifer Bassett
Founder Editor: Tricia Hedge
Activities Editors: Jennifer Bassett and Christine Lindop

NOTES ON THE ILLUSTRATORS

MESHACK ASARE (illustrations on pages 3, 7, 10, 14) was born in 1945 in Ghana. He studied Art, and later Social Anthropology, and was a teacher for many years. He is now a very well-known writer and illustrator of children's books, and travels widely through Africa looking for different African cultures to represent in his stories. His books have won numerous awards, including Noma and UNESCO awards, and have been published in many countries.

JOSEPH NTENSIBE (illustrations on pages 20, 25, 28) was born in 1951 in Uganda, East Africa. A freelance artist for many years, he works in oils, ink, pencil and charcoal, and watercolours, and his artworks have been shown in galleries in Kenya and the USA. These are his first book illustrations.

PETERSON KAMWATHI (illustrations on pages 35, 39) was born in 1980 in Nairobi, Kenya, and started painting after high school. He has had three solo art exhibitions, and taken part in many group exhibitions. These are his first book illustrations.

RETOLD BY JENNIFER BASSETT

Changing their Skies

Stories from Africa

OXFORD UNIVERSITY PRESS

OXFORD
UNIVERSITY PRESS

Great Clarendon Street, Oxford OX2 6DP

Oxford University Press is a department of the University of Oxford.
It furthers the University's objective of excellence in research, scholarship,
and education by publishing worldwide in

Oxford New York

Auckland Cape Town Dar es Salaam Hong Kong Karachi
Kuala Lumpur Madrid Melbourne Mexico City Nairobi
New Delhi Shanghai Taipei Toronto

With offices in

Argentina Austria Brazil Chile Czech Republic France Greece
Guatemala Hungary Italy Japan Poland Portugal Singapore
South Korea Switzerland Thailand Turkey Ukraine Vietnam

OXFORD and OXFORD ENGLISH are registered trade marks of
Oxford University Press in the UK and in certain other countries

Copyright of original texts:
The Rubbish Dump © Steve Chimombo 1984
Cardboard Mansions © Farida Karodia 1988
Leaving © M. G. Vassanji 1992

This simplified edition © Oxford University Press 2008

The moral rights of the author have been asserted

Database right Oxford University Press (maker)

First published in Oxford Bookworms 2008

17 16 15 14 13 12 11 10 9 8

No unauthorized photocopying

All rights reserved. No part of this publication may be reproduced,
stored in a retrieval system, or transmitted, in any form or by any means,
without the prior permission in writing of Oxford University Press,
or as expressly permitted by law, or under terms agreed with the appropriate
reprographics rights organization. Enquiries concerning reproduction
outside the scope of the above should be sent to the ELT Rights Department,
Oxford University Press, at the address above

You must not circulate this book in any other binding or cover
and you must impose this same condition on any acquirer

Any websites referred to in this publication are in the public domain and
their addresses are provided by Oxford University Press for information only.
Oxford University Press disclaims any responsibility for the content

ISBN: 978 0 19 479082 6

A complete recording of this Bookworms edition of *Changing their Skies:
Stories from Africa* is available.

Printed in China

ACKNOWLEDGEMENTS

The publishers are grateful to the following for permission to adapt and simplify copyright texts:
the author for 'The Rubbish Dump' by Steve Chimombo from *Namaluzi: Ten Stories from Malawi*
(Dzuka Publishing Co. 1984); the author for 'Cardboard Mansions' from *Coming Home and Other
Stories* by Farida Karodia (Harcourt Education Ltd 1988);
the author M. G. Vassanji and McClelland & Stewart Ltd for 'Leaving' from
Uhuru Street (McClelland & Stewart Ltd, 1992/Heinemann International Literature
and Textbooks, 1991). Copyright © 1992 M. G. Vassanji. With permission of the author.

Word count (main text): 6,987 words

For more information on the Oxford Bookworms Library,
visit www.oup.com/elt/gradedreaders

CONTENTS

NOTE ON THE LANGUAGE

There are many varieties of English spoken in the world, and the characters in these stories from Africa sometimes use non-standard forms (for example, leaving out auxiliary verbs such as *are*, *is*, *do*, *will*; and using double negatives such as *we don't do nothing*). This is how the authors of the original stories represented the spoken language that their characters would actually use in real life.

The Rubbish Dump

STEVE CHIMOMBO

A story from Malawi, retold by Jennifer Bassett

Rubbish is a problem in the rich world. There is too much of it, and people don't know what to do with it. In places like Africa there is less rubbish, because people have less to throw away.

An airport rubbish dump is a strange place, a meeting point for rubbish that has travelled a long way. It is also a meeting point for Joey and Mazambezi . . .

J oey sat on the ground, playing with a small toy car. The car was made out of bits and pieces – lots of old wire, pieces of cardboard, sticks, and the tops of baby-food cans for wheels.

Joey was working hard, his hands busily pulling and pushing pieces of wire which were not in the right places. After a moment, he put the car down with a pleased little grunt, and began to sing:

> *The white man is wise*
> *He made the aeroplane*
> *It's nothing else*
> *But determination.*

His high voice filled the air for a few minutes. Then came a louder noise – the squeak, rattle, and thump of a wheelbarrow along the road past the last row of houses. Joey's song stopped, started, stopped again. The wheelbarrow was getting nearer, and the squeak, rattle, and thump got louder and louder.

It was Mazambezi. The name meant 'rubbish collector', and that's what everyone called him – behind his back. Mazambezi, pushing his wheelbarrow, with the rubbish collected from the airport.

Joey stopped playing with his car, and looked unhappy. He remembered that today was Friday, and on Fridays the big aeroplane came in from London. People around the airport called it 'Four Engine'. Mazambezi was bringing in the rubbish from that plane, which meant it was now too late for Joey to run to the airport. He liked to go up to the balcony in the airport building and watch the passengers in their expensive clothes getting off the plane. They always carried bags and cameras, and strange and mysterious things from faraway countries. But it was too late to see them today. Perhaps the next passengers were already on the plane, ready to leave.

Then Joey heard the sound of aeroplane engines, and knew he was right. He stared at the sky. A moment later the rooftops of the houses began to rattle and the great silver plane went overhead in a terrible roar of engine noise.

*Joey heard the sound of aeroplane engines,
and stared at the sky.*

It was hard to live next to an international airport. Every time planes took off or landed, the airport workers' little houses shook and rattled. But Joey didn't mind. He loved the noise and the roar, and the cleverness that made those great machines fly like birds through the sky.

Soon the plane was gone. Joey still watched the sky, thinking. Who was on the plane today? Where was it going? To Salisbury, Johannesburg, and then on to England? One day, when he could read, he would find all those famous places in a book and learn about them.

The squeak, rattle, and thump of the wheelbarrow was very near now. Joey left his toy car and walked down to the road where Mazambezi was passing. The rubbish dump was only a hundred metres from his house.

'Hello, Joey,' the man said to Joey.

'Hello.' Joey stopped to watch the wheelbarrow pass.

'You haven't gone to school today?' Mazambezi asked.

'We've got a month's holiday.'

'That's good.'

'What have you got this time?' asked Joey.

'I don't know,' Mazambezi said. 'A few pieces of cheese and some vomit, maybe.'

Joey covered his nose with his hand when he heard the word 'vomit'. He knew that passengers on planes sometimes felt ill and that there were special bags for them to vomit into. Why did people vomit when they were flying in a plane? Sometimes Joey's father vomited, if he drank too much beer in the evenings. It wasn't very nice.

Joey followed the old man. He could never think of Mazambezi without his wheelbarrow – man and machine belonged together. The machine was old, and black with dirt and bits of old rubbish. Every part of the machine squeaked and rattled when it moved. The man too was old, with a lot of grey in his short black hair. His clothes were all bits and pieces, and full of holes; an old green and brown army hat kept the sun off his head.

They were nearly at the rubbish pit now, and Joey remembered his first meeting with Mazambezi and his first visit to the dump.

It was a week after his family moved into one of the little airport houses. Every day Joey saw Mazambezi go past with his wheelbarrow to the dump and then, later, go past again, going back to the airport. Why did he take so long to leave the rubbish? What did he do at the dump?

So one day Joey followed him. The terrible smell from the rubbish dump came along the road to meet him. It was like a cloud that filled his nose, his mouth, his head, his stomach. He saw Mazambezi sitting by the side of the pit, looking down into it. Joey went nearer, and then his foot hit something on the ground and he fell . . . into something soft and horrible.

He tried to get up, and a hand took his arm to help him.

'Are you all right?'

The old man's voice was coming out of the pit, Joey thought.

'Don't touch me!' he shouted angrily. 'You dirty old Mazambezi!'

The old man stepped back slowly. Joey got to his feet, turned, and ran. Halfway across the field to his house, he looked back. Mazambezi was looking through the rubbish in the wheelbarrow, finding bits of food left from the aeroplane meals. This was his lunch.

Back at home Joey looked at his dirty clothes and remembered the vomit. He went behind the kitchen and began to cry. His mother found him there. She looked at his clothes and knew at once.

'You've been to that smelly rubbish pit! You mustn't go there – you'll catch something horrible and get ill.'

So Joey was in trouble with his mother, and in more trouble with his father when he came home from work.

After that Joey spent his free time on the balcony at the airport. He learnt the times of all the planes, and he knew which plane was coming in, when, and where from. He also worked on his toy car, and when he got bored with that, he built himself an aeroplane. It wasn't very good and looked a bit like an old potato, but Joey flew it to Moscow, Tokyo, London, New York, and back.

*When Joey looked back, Mazambezi was looking through
the rubbish in the wheelbarrow.*

Mazambezi went past with his wheelbarrow every day as usual. Joey sometimes saw him because New York airport was on the road to the rubbish dump. One day Joey was talking to the man at Tokyo airport.

'Coming in to land. Can you hear me? Coming in to land. Can you hear me?' he said again and again. He knew the right words to say because his father told him what pilots said.

'Look, Joey,' a voice said behind him. 'I've got a real plane for you.'

It was Mazambezi. He was holding out a toy plane, with AIR RHODESIA written on the side. He looked at Joey with his sad brown eyes, and Joey looked back at him, afraid. He stepped back, away from the old man, then stepped forward again, took the toy plane, and ran home as fast as he could.

Near the house he stopped and hid the plane under his shirt. It looked very strange, and Joey crossed his arms in front of him, which looked even stranger. He walked into the house, singing,

> *The white man is wise*
> *He made the aeroplane*
> *It's nothing else*
> *But determination.*

Luckily, his mother was cleaning the big bedroom. Joey ran to the little room where he slept, and hid his AIR RHODESIA plane in his school bag. He kept all his secret things in there – foreign money, empty cigarette packets, all the things he found in the airport. He lay down on his sleeping mat and listened to his mother cleaning. Then his hand went into his school bag and brought out the little plane. It had a broken tail, but when he held it at the tail end, no one could see the broken bit.

'Joey, are you in there?'

'Yes, Mother,' Joey answered. Quickly, he pushed the plane back into his bag, and lay down again.

'What are you doing down there?' His mother was a big woman, and she filled the doorway.

'I – I have a headache, Mother.'

'Why didn't you tell me?'

'You were busy, Mother.'

'Too busy to tell me you are ill?'

'I – I –'

'Come here, Joey.'

'Yes, Mother.'

'Now, don't try and tell me you're sick, when you're not!' As usual, her finger was five centimetres away from his nose.

'No, Mother.'

'I saw you running around and singing a few minutes ago.'

'I – I – Mother –'

'Don't lie to me.'

'No, Mother.'

'Now, don't try and tell me that you're sick!' As usual,
her finger was five centimetres away from Joey's nose.

'Good. Now, I want you to go to the shop to get me some sugar and some tea. Here's the money.'

'Yes, Mother.'

Joey took the money and went out without a word. He was afraid that his mother would find the plane. He knew what she would say – Where did you get *that*, Joey? He ran to the shop and back as fast as he could.

'I thought you had a terrible headache,' his mother said when he got back.

'I – I – it's gone, Mother.'

'Good. Now, help me take the things out of your room. I need to clean it.'

Joey carried his school bag, his books, clothes, and sleeping mat out of the room, put them all in a corner, and stood over them. When his mother finished, he took his things carefully back into the room.

'You're very strange today.' His mother was looking hard at him. 'Are you sure your headache is gone?'

'No, Mother.' Joey did not look at her. 'It's come back.'

'Mmm. Maybe,' she said. 'You can lie down.'

Joey lay down again on his mat. He felt calmer now.

His father came home late that night, full of beer and singing noisily. Joey heard his voice in the kitchen, telling his mother about the white man.

'The white man is a nice man,' said Joey's father. 'The white man buys me drinks, he brings good things to the country – jobs, cars, aeroplanes. The white man is the African's friend . . .'

Joey's father was very boring when he was like this. His mother was now in the big bedroom, but Joey knew she was listening. Everybody in the house had to listen because his father talked so loudly.

It was a week before Joey was brave enough to go and meet Mazambezi on the road.

'Thank you for the plane,' he said to the old man.

Mazambezi gave a grunt that was lost in the squeak, rattle, thump of the wheelbarrow. Joey walked beside him down the road.

'What have you got this time?' he asked.

'Some pieces of meat, with the usual things.'

Joey tried not to think about the 'usual things'. The man and Joey turned the corner, and the smell of the pit came strongly towards them.

The pit was very old and large, but not deep. Many other people used it, not just Mazambezi. Office workers brought their banana skins, chicken bones, fish bones – if people did not want something, they threw it into the pit. The flies buzzed angrily over it all, and in the sky above big black birds circled, calling loudly. Down in the pit, under the rubbish, lived other kinds of life.

Joey looked at all the empty milk, fish, and meat cans lying in the pit.

'Did all that come from the plane?' he asked.

'Yes.'

'They must eat a lot.'

'When the white man eats, he eats.' Mazambezi picked up a can from the edge of the pit. 'Where do you think this can came from?' he said.

'London?'

'No.'

'Paris?'

'No. It was made in Hong Kong,' Mazambezi said. 'I sit here every day and look into the pit. I pick up meat cans or fish cans and think about the places where they came from. Japan? Russia? England? America? South Africa? All the world is open to me.' He sounded excited. 'How many thousands of miles has this can of fish travelled? Who didn't eat their piece of cheese? What language do they speak? What hopes and dreams do they have? I don't need to ride in their planes. I sit here, and Russia, America, Hong Kong, England all come to me. They all find their way into this rubbish dump.'

'I do the same,' Joey said quickly, 'when I go to the balcony to watch the planes come and go. Every day at school, when I open my books, I hope that one day I can read all about these places. Perhaps even visit them. Walking in the streets of London or New York or Tokyo – just imagine it!'

'I know how you feel,' Mazambezi said.

'Here,' the old man said, 'have a piece of cheese.
Maybe it came from South Africa.'

'But I've also seen the places.' Joey's eyes were shining.

'Have you?'

'Yes. Every day, when I fly the plane that you gave me, I see them so clearly. I drink Coca-Cola in New York, have tea in London, and go for a drive in Tokyo.'

They sat at the edge of the dump, with their legs hanging down into the pit, and looked at the broken bottles made in England, empty food cans made in the USA, and plastic bags made in Japan. Each thought his own thoughts. The smells of the rubbish were all around them; the black birds circled above them, and the endless buzzing of the flies rang in their ears.

'Here,' the old man said, 'have a piece of cheese. Maybe it came from South Africa.'

Joey took the cheese and began to eat it. He put his back against the wheelbarrow, getting comfortable.

After a while they heard the noise of aeroplane engines.

'It's the "Four Engine",' Joey said.

'Yes, it's the big plane taking off.'

'Will it stop in Salisbury?'

'Maybe.'

'Who's in it?'

'Oh, the usual. Rich fat white men, brown men, and a few blacks.'

'Students going for more education.'

'Yes, I forgot about those.' Mazambezi stood up with a grunt. 'I've got to go now too.'

'Goodbye,' said Joey slowly. He too stood up. 'We'll meet again tomorrow?'

'Yes.' The old man began to push his wheelbarrow and they went away down the road – the squeak, rattle, and thump of the machine, and the silent man.

Joey watched them go. Who will die first, he thought, man or machine? But not yet. For now, Joey knew that everything would stay the same. Every day there would be the same question and the same answer:

'What has the big plane brought today?'

'Oh, bits and pieces from the white man's land.'

The rubbish would find its way to the dump; the flies and the birds; Mazambezi and Joey.

Cardboard Mansions

FARIDA KARODIA

A story from South Africa, retold by Jennifer Bassett

Most people don't live in mansions; those are great houses for the very rich. Lucky people have houses with clean water, without bad smells, and with walls that keep out the sound of neighbours shouting. Unlucky people have only shanties to live in – houses made out of bits of old metal or cardboard or paper.

And some people only have dreams . . .

'Chotoo! Eh, Chotoo!'

'Yes, Dadi-Ma?' the boy cried from the far side of the yard.

'Don't just say yes, boy! Come here!' the old woman called. She tried to look over the low wall and round the corner of the building, but there was a big pile of rubbish there and she could not see over it. She stepped back into the doorway, away from the rubbish pile.

She waited for the boy, pulling the end of her old green cotton sari over her head. Her wide, flat feet nearly hid her sandals, which were much too small for her.

Dadi-Ma looked much older than her seventy-three years. She was a tall heavy woman, who moved slowly.

Dark brown eyes stared out of a face which was deeply lined, and each line told a story of a long, hard life.

These days there was no one left who remembered Dadi-Ma as a beautiful young woman, with shining dark eyes. Her only family was Sonny, her youngest son, and Chotoo, her grandson. Her husband and three of her sons, like so many of the workers in the sugar-cane fields, were dead, killed by the disease of tuberculosis.

And now the only people in her life were her grandchild, Chotoo, and her friend Ratnadevi. Dadi-Ma, old and tired, was left to watch the world go by.

The boy, Chotoo, took a long time coming. His grandmother waited, standing in the doorway.

'Chotoo!' she called again, then sat down on the step to wait.

The shanty houses were really just one long building. It was once a kind of factory, but the owner, Mr Naidoo, put up thin walls inside the building and made little homes. All the walls stopped about thirty centimetres short of the ceiling and the 'homes' were just one room, not much bigger than a large box. But poor people have to live somewhere.

Everybody could hear everything over the tops of the walls. When a man beat his wife on a Saturday night, her cries sounded all through the building, and everybody had to listen. Dadi-Ma often said to Neela, Sonny's wife,

'Well, Sonny doesn't beat you, that's one good thing.'

But Sonny was not a good husband, or a good son, or a good father. He didn't beat his wife, but he often beat little Chotoo. Then, three years ago, Neela died. And not long after that Sonny lost his job.

Life was difficult then. There was no money coming in to pay the rent, and Mr Naidoo did not like waiting for his rent money. There were often angry words between Sonny and Mr Naidoo.

Life got more and more difficult. Sonny drank a lot and started smoking all kinds of things – things that made him crazy. When he was like that, Dadi-Ma and Chotoo had to hide from him.

Then one day it happened. Sonny drank too much, got into a fight, and used his knife on someone. The police arrested him, and soon Sonny was in prison. After that it was just Dadi-Ma and Chotoo in their little shanty home.

One way or another, Dadi-Ma found a little money to pay some of the rent. But each week she paid less and less, and got more and more behind with her rent. In the end Mr Naidoo told her to go.

'I want four months' rent by the end of the week,' he said. 'If you don't pay, you go. Out. You and the boy.'

Dadi-Ma was very unhappy about this. What could she do? They had to move, but where to? She did not worry for herself because she did not have many more years left

*Chotoo sat down on the step next to Dadi-Ma, sitting close
to her side, where he felt safe and comfortable.*

to live. But what about the boy, who was just five years old and only starting out in life?

'What took you so long, hey?' Dadi-Ma asked, when the boy at last came to find her.

He pushed his hands deep into his pockets, and stood with his legs apart, trying to look like one of the older boys from the shanty houses. Dadi-Ma pulled his hair gently, and he sat down on the step next to her, sitting close to her side, where he felt safe and comfortable.

For a time they sat there silently, the boy happy to be close to her, and his grandmother thinking about the past, and the future with its worries and its problems.

'Why you like those boys from the shanties?' Dadi-Ma asked her grandson. 'They no good.'

'Why you say that, Dadi-Ma?' he asked. His big brown eyes looked up at her, surprised.

He was so young, she thought. How could he understand? She wanted him to do something with his life, to escape from life in the shanties.

'Because they bad. They drink, they smoke. You best go to school, and then you can be something, hey?'

'We don't do nothing wrong, Dadi-Ma. We just sit out there, and talk and laugh,' said the boy.

The old woman shook her head tiredly.

'They say old man Naidoo going to throw us out,' the boy went on. 'Where we going to go, Dadi-Ma?'

Dadi-Ma felt a strong love for her grandson. Right from the day he was born, he was her boy, her little Chotoo. His mother, Neela, was too ill and tired to take care of her baby, and so Dadi-Ma was both mother and father to the child. She did not show her love in words, just pulled Chotoo's hair gently, or touched his cheek.

The boy, small for his years, and with the same big brown eyes as his grandmother, knew that she loved him. Other people in his life, like his parents, went away and never came back. But not her. Dadi-Ma was the centre of his little life, the rock that did not move, the place where he was safe and loved.

'I was thinking, Chotoo, maybe you and me, we go to Stanger,' the old woman said quietly. 'It will be a good place for us. This place is no good.'

'Where is Stanger, Dadi-Ma?' he asked, excitedly.

'It's not so far away.'

'How will we go . . . by car, by train?' he asked, in his high little voice.

She smiled down at him. 'We go by train.'

Dadi-Ma had a little money, fifty rands, hidden in a secret place – money saved from the good old days when Sonny had a job, money saved for bad times. And now those bad times were here.

Dadi-Ma looked down at Chotoo. 'You don't tell nobody,' she said. 'Be careful. If old man Naidoo finds out, he make big trouble for us.'

'Yes.' Chotoo understood this, even at five years old. 'Can I go and play now, Dadi-Ma?'

'Yes, you go and play. But remember.'

'I won't tell nobody, Dadi-Ma.'

He walked away, and Dadi-Ma watched his thin legs and his bony feet, hard and dirty from going barefoot. She began to think again about Stanger, and the past, and her friend Ratnadevi.

She and Ratnadevi were young women when they arrived in South Africa from India all those years ago. They came on the same boat to marry Indian workers in the sugar-cane fields in Natal. They lived in the same building with all the other workers. It was a hard life, but the two young women were as close as sisters, always together, during the happy times and the sad times.

When her husband died, Ratnadevi moved to Stanger, a town further north on the east coast. And when Dadi-Ma's husband died and young Sonny left home, Dadi-Ma also moved to Stanger to live with Ratnadevi.

Oh, those were happy years in Stanger! She remembered it all so clearly. The little wooden house on the edge of town, the last house on the street, at the end of a dirt road . . . That big garden, with all those fruit trees, bananas, mangoes – so much fruit! There was enough even for the birds.

She and Ratnadevi worked hard, but they were happy.

They took in washing from the white people's houses – the garden was always full of clothes and sheets drying in the sun. They made baskets to sell, they had chickens and sold eggs in the market every day. They were poor, but they were not hungry. They could sit outside in the clean air, and see the hills to the north, and watch the brightly coloured birds flying in and out of the fruit trees. It was a good life.

And then it all changed. Sonny, now with a new wife and living in Port Elizabeth, sent for her. When a son calls you, you have to go. Dadi-Ma packed her small bag and went to live with Sonny and Neela, his new wife. Neela was just a young girl, who was always ill and could not work or do anything. Dadi-Ma took care of them all.

Neela was a difficult person, and Dadi-Ma hated living in a city. The years went by and her time at Stanger got further and further away, but she did not forget. Then one day, five years ago, Chotoo was born – and brought new meaning into Dadi-Ma's life.

Dadi-Ma sat on the step, thinking of that little wooden house in Stanger. She could almost see the fruit trees, and the birds flying in and out.

Around her the smells of the shanty houses were as strong as ever – the smells of people, smoke, dirt, rubbish, cooking, unwashed bodies . . .

It was good they were leaving, Dadi-Ma thought. The

They made baskets to sell, they had chickens and sold eggs . . .
They were poor, but they were not hungry.

boy needed to run free, to breathe clean air. She smiled to herself and thought about sitting out in the yard again with Ratnadevi, making baskets, talking, laughing.

That night she put all their things into a small bundle, and she and Chotoo left very quietly, when it was dark. She did not want Mr Naidoo to see them and start asking for his rent.

They caught the train for Durban early next morning. For Chotoo it was a big adventure. All through the journey he stood by the window, with his nose against the glass. In the crowds at Durban station he held on to Dadi-Ma's sari and stayed close by her side. Outside the station they found the bus for Stanger and got in.

It was a long drive, past field after field of sugar-cane. Chotoo again stood with his nose against the window, watching everything. The bus stopped often, and it was afternoon before they arrived at Stanger.

The bus drove into the town and Dadi-Ma looked around, but everything was different. Where was the market? Where was the bus-stop? She asked someone sitting near them, but they did not know. 'The woman at the front of the bus lives here. Ask her,' they said.

So Dadi-Ma went to talk to the woman at the front of the bus. 'Stay here,' she said to Chotoo, 'keep our seat.'

Dadi-Ma spoke to the woman for several minutes. Chotoo, watching, began to feel worried.

'What is it, Dadi-Ma?' he said, when she came back.

'We will have to walk a long way,' she told him.

'Why?' he asked.

'So many questions!' said Dadi-Ma. 'The market is in a new place . . . and they have moved the bus-stop. So it is a long walk now to our street.'

The boy did not say anything; but he knew that Dadi-Ma was worried, and he felt a little frightened.

When they got off the bus, the woman from the front of the bus came to talk to them.

'Why do you want to go to that street?' she asked.

'My friend Ratnadevi lives there,' said Dadi-Ma. 'She has a small house with big trees.'

The woman looked at her, surprised. Then she explained again to Dadi-Ma how to get to the street. When she finished, she said, 'But there is no small house there. They are all big houses.'

Dadi-Ma smiled and thanked the woman. 'When I get there, I will know where to go,' she said.

She put her bundle onto her head. Chotoo held on to her sari with his hand, and they started walking.

They walked a long way, stopping often to rest. Soon Chotoo was tired, and Dadi-Ma talked to him about the fruit trees and the birds. They turned left, walked down a long, long road, then turned right, and right again. Sometimes Dadi-Ma remembered a building or a street from the past, but many of the buildings were new.

One more turn, and at last they were in the right place.

*They began to walk down the street. On both sides
were large houses behind high walls.*

They began to walk down the street. On both sides were large houses behind high walls. Dadi-Ma's dark eyes stared around her; it was all new and strange. Slowly, they went to the end of the street, but Ratnadevi's house was no longer there. There were no fruit trees, no birds calling and flying in and out of the trees. Dadi-Ma took the bundle off her head. She was tired and her legs were shaking. She sat down by the side of the road, pulling the boy close to her side.

'What's wrong, Dadi-Ma? Where's Ratnadevi's house?'

Dadi-Ma's fingers were moving, in and out, in and out, making something that no one could see. A basket, maybe . . . one of the baskets she and Ratnadevi once made, all those years ago.

'Dadi-Ma?' Chotoo said in a small voice.

'Hush, Chotoo. Don't worry. We'll rest a bit and then we'll find Ratnadevi's house.'

Chotoo was tired and sleepy; he sat closer to his grandmother's side, and rested his head on her arm.

Maybe this was the wrong street, thought Dadi-Ma. Yes, Ratnadevi's house was at the end of some other street, and in a while she would find it. A small wooden house with fruit trees around it. Chotoo could climb trees and pick fruit, and eat as much as he wanted. He could help them with the baskets.

Then a woman came out of one of the big houses and

came up to them. 'Why are you sitting here?' she asked.

Dadi-Ma said she was looking for a friend, and described Ratnadevi's house.

'Yes, I remember that house,' the woman said. 'They pulled it down a long time ago.'

'What happened to the people who lived there?' Dadi-Ma asked.

'I don't know,' the woman said.

Dadi-Ma felt so tired, so tired. Now she could feel a pain inside her body, and all down her arms. The colour in her face changed, and the woman saw it.

'Are you all right, Auntie?' she asked.

Dadi-Ma did not answer. She did not want Chotoo to be frightened. Slowly, she tried to stand up, the woman helping her.

But Chotoo saw Dadi-Ma's face, and for the first time in his life he was really afraid – afraid for the future, afraid of losing Dadi-Ma. She was the only person in his life, the only person who loved him.

'Dadi-Ma, Dadi-Ma,' he sobbed.

'It's all right, Chotoo, it's all right.'

But Chotoo knew that it wasn't all right. He knew that it would never be all right again.

Leaving

M. G. VASSANJI

A story from Tanzania, retold by Jennifer Bassett

Every mother wants her children to be happy, to have a good education, to do well in life. But children grow up, and some mothers find it hard to let them go.

It is natural for children to leave home, to look for excitement, to start their own lives, free from their parents. But to leave, and never return . . .?

Kichwele Street was now Uhuru Street. My two sisters got married, and Mother was sad to see them leave home. Mehroon and her husband lived in town, but Razia was a rich housewife in Tanga, a town on the coast north of Dar es Salaam. Firoz, my older brother, did not finish his last year at school, and no one was surprised at that. He was working in the office of a big shop.

Mother's hopes were now on the youngest two of us, Aloo and me. She wanted us to study hard and not to spend time working in our store. So one evening she locked up the big doors for the last time, and sold the store. That was just one week after Razia got married.

We moved to a part of town called Upanga, which was a very quiet place after the noise and hurry of Uhuru Street. We no longer heard the sounds of buses, cars, and bicycles; we heard the sounds of insects and small animals, of leaves rustling in the wind. There were only a few houses in Upanga at that time, and behind the houses was wild land, with tall trees. There were no streetlights, and at night it felt a lonely, frightening place.

Sometimes in the evenings, when Mother felt sad, Aloo and I played card games with her. By now I was at university, living there during the week and coming home at weekends. Aloo was in his last year at school. He was a clever student – in fact, much cleverer than we knew.

That year Mr Datoo, who was once a teacher at our school, came back from America for a visit. He was a favourite with the boys, who were all pleased to see him. For the next few days he went round the town followed by a great group of boys. One of them was Aloo.

It was because of Mr Datoo's visit that Aloo began to think about his future. Could he perhaps get into an American university? Of course, it was expensive, but could he perhaps win a scholarship to pay for it? All through the rest of that year he wrote to universities in America, finding their names in books.

Mother just smiled at all this busy letter-writing. 'Oh yes,' she often said, 'your uncles in America will pay money just to send you to college. Oh yes!'

We all knew that was not true, of course. Mother just didn't take Aloo's plan seriously.

Some weeks later answers to the letters began arriving, with big shiny prospectuses. Slowly, Aloo learnt which universities were good, which were famous, which were the best for this or that subject. He learnt that people could study all kinds of strange and interesting things – an exciting new world was waiting for him out there. But could he get there? Was he good enough?

Of course, Aloo had a place at our own university. At the end of the year his name was on the list – but it was not what he wanted. He wanted to study medicine, but they gave him a place to study agriculture. Aloo was not interested in farms or farming; he wanted to live and work in a city. But nobody could change the list.

Then a letter came for Aloo from the California Institute of Technology, a famous college in America. They offered him a place . . . a place with a scholarship. Aloo could not believe it at first. He read the letter again and again. Then he asked me to read it. When he was sure there was no mistake, he was so happy.

'Agriculture?' he laughed. 'They can forget it!'

But first he had to talk to Mother.

Mother did not believe him. 'Go away,' she said. 'Stop playing games with me!'

'But it's true!' Aloo said. 'They're giving me a place with a scholarship.'

The three of us were at the table, drinking tea. Mother stared down at her tea for a while, then she looked up.

'Is it true?' she asked me.

'Yes, it's true,' I said. 'He only needs to take four hundred dollars spending money with him.'

'How many shillings would that be?' she asked.

'About three thousand.'

'And how are we going to get three thousand shillings? And what about the plane ticket? Are they going to send you a ticket too?'

Aloo's hopes began to look unreal. She was right; he would need much more money than that.

'Can't we borrow some money?' he asked. 'I'll work in America. Yes, I'll work in a restaurant or something – I know students can do that. I'll send the money back!'

'Maybe you have uncles in America who will help you,' Mother told him, 'but no one here will.'

Aloo looked unhappy, and he sat there, staring at the table. Mother drank her tea slowly, thinking. Then she put her tea down. She was angry.

'And why do you want to go away, so far from us? What kind of son are you? You want to leave me and go away to a foreign place? Won't you miss us? Are we so unimportant to you? If something happens . . .'

Aloo was crying. 'So many kids go and return, and nothing happens to them . . . Why did you let me write to all these places if you didn't want me to go? Why did you

'And why do you want to go away, so far from us?
What kind of son are you?'

let me hope?' He was shouting at her, the only time I ever heard him do that, and he was shaking.

He did not speak about it again, and he prepared himself for agricultural college. While he waited for the college year to begin, he just read novels, lying in a chair at home, reading for hours and hours.

Mother was not made of stone. She knew how Aloo felt about studying agriculture.

A few days later, on a Sunday morning, she looked up from her sewing machine and said to the two of us: 'Let's go and show this letter to Mr Velji. He understands things like these. Let's take his advice.'

Mr Velji was one of our school officers. He had a large head, which looked like an egg, and a small neat body. He wore big black glasses, and looked like a clever man. We sat in his sitting-room, waiting for him.

He walked in like a soldier and welcomed us. Aloo and I stood up politely.

'How are you?' he said to Mother. 'What can I do for you?'

'We have come to you for advice . . .' Mother began.

'Speak, then,' he said smiling, and sat back to listen.

Mother told him all about our family, about our father's death, and what all her older children were doing. 'And now,' she said, pointing at Aloo, 'this one wants to go to America. Aloo, show him the documents.'

Aloo put all the papers into Mr Velji's hands.

'How did you do in the school exam?' Mr Velji asked.

At Aloo's answer, Mr Velji's eyes opened very wide. 'All A's?' he asked.

'Yes,' said Aloo.

Mr Velji read the papers carefully – the long visa form, the friendly letter from the Foreign Student Adviser, the letters of welcome from the student houses. At last he looked up.

'The boy is right,' he said. 'The university is good, and they are giving him a scholarship. It is a great thing.'

'But what must I do?' asked Mother, worried. 'What is your advice? Tell us what we must do.'

'Well,' said Mr Velji, 'it will be good for his education.' He stopped, then went on, a little slowly. 'But if you send him, you will lose your son . . . It is a far place, America.'

When we walked back home, Aloo whispered angrily, 'All the rich kids go every year and they are not lost.' Mother was silent.

That night she was at the sewing machine and Aloo was reading. Through the open front door a little wind came in, bringing some welcome cool air into the hot room. I was standing at the door, listening to the night sounds – trees rustling, voices from young people in the street, calling goodnight to their friends.

After a while Mother looked up and said, without any great interest in her voice, 'Well, show me what this university looks like – bring that prospectus, will you?'

The three of us sat down to look at the prospectus. We turned the shiny pages, looking at the pictures of tall, grand buildings, students hurrying here and there, classes taking place outside, under the shade of trees. It all looked so wonderful.

'It's something, isn't it?' whispered Aloo. He could not hide the excitement in his voice. 'They teach everything there,' he said. 'They send rockets to the moon . . .'

'If you go away to the moon, my son, what will happen to me?' Mother asked, smiling.

Aloo went back to his book and Mother to her sewing machine.

A little later I looked up and saw Mother's face. She was thinking deeply. That was the first time I saw her as a person, and not just as our mother. When Father died, she was only thirty-three. It was a hard life, with five children and no husband. In the years after his death several men asked her to marry them, but she always refused to marry again, because of us. Children of a first marriage cannot stay with their mother in a second marriage; they are sent to a children's home.

There were pictures of Mother before Father died. They showed her smiling and pretty, wearing beautiful clothes. I never knew her when she was like that. I knew only a worried, unsmiling face, a face with deep lines getting deeper every year, hair getting thinner, a body getting fatter, a voice no longer soft.

Aloo could not hide the excitement in his voice. 'They teach everything there,' he said.

I remembered her arms around me when I was a young child. I remembered it was difficult to breathe because she held me so close.

She looked at me looking at her and said, not to me, 'Promise me . . . promise me that if I let you go, you will not marry a white woman.'

'Oh Mother, you know I won't!' said Aloo.

'And promise me that you will not smoke or drink.'

'You know I promise!' He was almost crying.

Aloo's first letter came a week after he left, from London. He stopped there to visit an old friend from school. The letter was full of excitement.

'How can I describe,' he wrote, 'what I saw from the plane? Mile after mile of green fields, neat green squares, even the mountains are clean and tidy. And London . . . Oh London! It never ends . . . houses, squares, parks, gardens, great buildings . . . How can any city be so big? How many of our Dar es Salaams would go into this one, beautiful city . . .?'

A bird flying high and free; Mr Velji sitting in his chair, his wise face full of understanding; Mother staring into the future.

GLOSSARY

advice words that you say to help somebody decide what to do

agriculture the science of farming (keeping animals and growing plants for food)

balcony a platform on the outside wall of a building, where you can stand or sit

barefoot with no shoes on your feet

basket a container made of thin sticks, that you use for holding or carrying things

believe to feel sure that something is true

bone one of the hard white parts inside the body

breathe to take air in through your nose and mouth

bundle a group of things that you tie together

buzz *(v)* to make the sound that insects like bees, flies, etc. make

can *(n)* a metal container for food or drink

cardboard very thick paper that is used for making boxes, etc.

cheek one of the two soft parts of the face below the eyes

cheese a yellow or white food made from milk

collector a person who collects things (e.g. rubbish, tickets)

college a place where people study after they have left school

dirt something that is not clean

document an official paper with important information on it

dump a place where people take things they do not want

education teaching and learning, in school, colleges, etc.

exam a test of what you know or what you can do

grunt *(n)* to make a short rough sound, like a pig makes

hang to let something fall downwards

horrible very bad or unpleasant

imagine to make a picture of something in your mind

international connected with many different countries

kid a child or young person

lined (of skin on the face) having lines or folds because of age

mat something that covers a part of the floor

medicine the science of understanding illnesses and making sick people well again

novel a book that tells a story about people and things that are not real

pile a lot of things on top of one another

pit a hole in the ground

plastic an artificial material that is used for making many different things (chairs, cups, bottles, etc.)

prospectus a book that gives information about a school, college, etc.

rent *(n)* the money that you pay to live in someone's house

roar *(n)* a loud deep sound

rubbish things that you do not want any more

sandal a light open shoe

sari a long piece of material that women (often Indian women) wear as a dress

scholarship money given to a good student to help them to continue studying

sewing machine a machine used for sewing and making clothes

shanty a small house, built of pieces of wood, cardboard, etc., where very poor people live

sob to cry loudly and very unhappily

squeak, rattle, thump three different sounds (the kinds of sounds made by machines)

store *(n)* a shop

sugar-cane a tall plant with thick stems from which sugar is made

throw (somebody) out to make somebody leave a place

toy a thing for a child to play with

tuberculosis a bad illness of the lungs, which often kills people

visa an official document to show that you can go into a country

vomit *(n & v)* the food that comes up from your stomach when you are sick

wheelbarrow a container with wheels that is pushed along the ground

wire a long piece of very thin metal

wise knowing and understanding a lot about many things

yard an area next to a building, usually with a wall around it

ACTIVITIES

Before Reading

Before you read the stories, read the introductions at the beginning. Then use these activities to help you think about the stories. How much can you guess about them?

1 *The Rubbish Dump* (story introduction page 1). Choose answers to these questions.

   1 Why do Joey and Mazambezi meet at the rubbish dump?

   a) Because it is a nice place to meet.

   b) Because Mazambezi is a rubbish collector and he works at the dump.

   2 Joey is a small boy and Mazambezi is an old man. What do they talk about when they meet?

   a) The things in the dump and where they came from.

   b) All the foreign countries that they have both visited.

   3 Why does Joey like to collect things from the airport?

   a) Because these things are his 'toys'.

   b) Because he is a thief.

2 *Cardboard Mansions* (story introduction page 17). Which ending do you think will be best for these sentences?

   1 The people in this story live in . . .

   a) a mansion.   b) a shanty.   c) a small house.

2 They need money to . . .

  a) pay the rent.   b) go on holiday.   c) buy a car.

3 They dream about living in . . .

  a) prison.   b) New York.   c) a house with a garden.

3 *Leaving* (story introduction page 31). Do you agree (A) or disagree (D) with these ideas?

  1 When children grow up, mothers should not try to keep them at home if they want to leave.

  2 Children should not move to another country if their parents need them at home.

  3 A good education is very important.

  4 A good education is the most important thing in life.

  5 It is better to go to university in your own country.

4 Which of these words do you think you will find in each story? Put the words into groups after each story title.

building	garden	smell
college	horrible	university
dirt	plastic	visa
exam	rent	wall

The Rubbish Dump: _____

Cardboard Mansions: _____

Leaving: _____

ACTIVITIES

After Reading

1 Perhaps one day Joey's mother found the little toy aeroplane in Joey's school bag. Here is her conversation with Joey. Write in the speakers' names, and put the conversation in the right order. Joey's mother speaks first (number 3).

1 _____ 'What do you mean, you don't know? Did you steal it?'

2 _____ 'He . . . the man with the wheelbarrow.'

3 _____ 'Joey! What's this that I found in your school bag?'

4 _____ 'No, I didn't! Someone gave it to me.'

5 _____ 'So it came from that smelly rubbish pit! Go and throw it away at once, Joey!'

6 _____ 'It's a toy aeroplane, Mother.'

7 _____ 'What wheelbarrow? Oh, you mean Mazambezi?'

8 _____ 'I – I – I don't know where it came from.'

9 _____ 'I can see it's an aeroplane! Where did it come from?'

10 _____ 'Yes.'

11 _____ 'Who? Come on, who gave it to you?'

2 **What do you think Joey did next? Choose one of these.**

1 He threw the toy aeroplane into the rubbish pit.

2 He hid it in a much more secret place.

3 **Use these clues to complete the crossword with words from the stories. All the words go across.**

1 Dadi-Ma did not have enough money to pay the _____.

2 Joey made a toy car out of wire and _____.

3 Mazambezi collected _____ in his wheelbarrow.

4 Aloo wanted to study _____ at university.

5 A college offered Aloo a place with a _____.

6 Joey and Mazambezi sat on the edge of the _____.

7 Aloo's mother went to Mr Velji for _____.

8 Chotoo had no shoes so he went _____.

9 Dadi-Ma and Chotoo lived in a _____.

Now find the hidden word of 9 letters in the crossword.

1 What is the word?

2 This thing is important to people in all three of the stories. Can you say how?

4 In the story *Leaving* what do you think will happen to Aloo in America? Here are three letters – one from Aloo to his mother, and two different replies from his mother. Use these words to complete all the letters (one word for each gap).

bring, broken, exams, few, girl, green, job, life, married, marry, meet, name, pleased, promised, red, top, understand, white

Dear Mother,

After five years, I have at last finished my studies. My _____ went well and I came _____ in my class! I know I _____ to come home when I finished, but a big hospital here has offered me a _____ . I will learn a lot working in an American hospital, so I must stay here for a _____ more years. And there's another thing. I know you won't like this, but I have met a _____. She's lovely! She has _____ hair and _____ eyes, and she comes from Ireland. Her _____ is Jacky. We want to get _____ next year. Please try to _____, Mother. I have to live my own _____.

   Love to all my brothers and sisters, and to you. Aloo

Reply 1

Dear Aloo, you have _____ my heart. You promised me that you would come home, and that you would not _____ a _____ woman. I will never speak to you again. Mother

Reply 2

Dear Aloo, top in your class, and a job in a hospital – that's wonderful! And I'm so _____ you've met a nice girl. Jacky sounds very beautiful. Why don't you _____ her here for a little holiday? We'd love to _____ her. All my love, Mother

5 **Read the two replies again, and answer these questions.**

1 Which reply do you think Aloo's mother will send?

2 Which reply do you think she *should* send? Why?

6 **What happens after the end of *Cardboard Mansions*? Here are two possible endings. Complete them in your own words. (Use as many words as you like.)**

1 Dadi-Ma died in the street a few minutes later. The woman from the big house _____ and Chotoo _____. Then the police came and _____. They sent Chotoo to _____. People were not _____ and he had a hard life.

2 The woman from the big house took Dadi-Ma and Chotoo _____ and gave them _____. They stayed there for _____. Dadi-Ma got _____ and Chotoo went _____. He learnt _____ and later he got _____. He took care of _____ until _____.

7 **Read the two endings again, and answer these questions.**

1 Which ending do you think is right for the story?

2 Which ending do you like best? Why?

8 Here is a short poem (a kind of poem called a haiku) about one of the stories. Which of the three stories is it about?

> *Will the travellers*
> *find the house she remembers?*
> *The end is unsure.*

Here is another haiku, about the same story.

> *He has no parents,*
> *no home, no shoes, but he has*
> *a grandmother's love.*

A haiku is a Japanese poem, which is always in three lines, and the three lines always have 5, 7, and 5 syllables each, like this:

| He | has | no | par | ents | = 5 syllables

| no | home | no | shoes | but | he | has | = 7 syllables

| a | grand | mo | ther's | love | = 5 syllables

Now write your own haiku, one for each of the other two stories. Think about what each story is really about. What are the important ideas for you? Remember to keep to three lines of 5, 7, 5 syllables each.

ABOUT THE AUTHORS

STEVE CHIMOMBO

Steve Chimombo (1945–) was born in Zomba, Malawi, and was educated at the University of Malawi, and then at universities in England and the United States. Until his retirement, he was Professor of English at Chancellor College, University of Malawi, and he has been a major figure in Malawi's literary circles for more than twenty years. He is a well-known poet, and his six volumes of poetry include *Napolo and the Python* (1994). He has also written plays, including *The Rainmaker* (1975) and *Sister! Sister!* (1995); novels, including *The Wrath of Napolo* (2000); several children's books; and collections of short stories, which include *The Hyena Wears Darkness* (2006). In an interview he has said that the main purpose of all his writing has been to show 'the cyclical nature of things, the rhythms of life, night and day, birth, death . . .'

FARIDA KARODIA

Farida Karodia was born in the Eastern Cape province in South Africa, into a cross-cultural family with an Indian father and a South African mother. She was a teacher in Johannesburg and later in Zambia, but when the South African government cancelled her passport in 1968, she emigrated to Canada. There she wrote radio plays, and in 1986 published her first novel, *Daughters of the Twilight*. In 1994, after the end of apartheid, she returned to South Africa. Her novels include *Other Secrets* (2000) and *Boundaries* (2003), and she has published two collections of short stories, *Coming Home and Other Stories*

(1988) and *Against an African Sky and Other Stories* (1995). An interviewer once asked her why she was a writer. 'I've never thought about why I write,' she said. 'I just know that it's something I have to do. I can't stop writing.'

M. G. VASSANJI

M. G. Vassanji (1950–) was born in Nairobi, Kenya, to an Indian family, and brought up in Tanzania. He now lives in Toronto, Canada, and visits Africa and India often. He studied at the Massachusetts Institute of Technology and the University of Pennsylvania in the USA, then moved to Canada in 1978. After the success of his first novel, *The Gunny Sack* (1989), he became a full-time writer, and so far has written six novels, and two collections of short stories, *Uhuru Street* (1990) and *When She Was Queen* (2005). His work has won several prizes, and deals with Indians living in East Africa. He says: 'Once I went to the US, suddenly the Indian connection became very important; the sense of origins, trying to understand the roots of India that we had inside us.'

OXFORD BOOKWORMS LIBRARY

Classics • Crime & Mystery • Factfiles • Fantasy & Horror
Human Interest • Playscripts • Thriller & Adventure
True Stories • World Stories

The OXFORD BOOKWORMS LIBRARY provides enjoyable reading in English, with a wide range of classic and modern fiction, non-fiction, and plays. It includes original and adapted texts in seven carefully graded language stages, which take learners from beginner to advanced level. An overview is given on the next pages.

All Stage 1 titles are available as audio recordings, as well as over eighty other titles from Starter to Stage 6. All Starters and many titles at Stages 1 to 4 are specially recommended for younger learners. Every Bookworm is illustrated, and Starters and Factfiles have full-colour illustrations.

The OXFORD BOOKWORMS LIBRARY also offers extensive support. Each book contains an introduction to the story, notes about the author, a glossary, and activities. Additional resources include tests and worksheets, and answers for these and for the activities in the books. There is advice on running a class library, using audio recordings, and the many ways of using Oxford Bookworms in reading programmes. Resource materials are available on the website <www.oup.com/elt/gradedreaders>.

The *Oxford Bookworms Collection* is a series for advanced learners. It consists of volumes of short stories by well-known authors, both classic and modern. Texts are not abridged or adapted in any way, but carefully selected to be accessible to the advanced student.

You can find details and a full list of titles in the *Oxford Bookworms Library Catalogue* and *Oxford English Language Teaching Catalogues*, and on the website <www.oup.com/elt/gradedreaders>.

THE OXFORD BOOKWORMS LIBRARY
GRADING AND SAMPLE EXTRACTS

STARTER • 250 HEADWORDS

present simple – present continuous – imperative –
can/cannot, must – going to (future) – simple gerunds ...

Her phone is ringing – but where is it?

Sally gets out of bed and looks in her bag. No phone. She looks under the bed. No phone. Then she looks behind the door. There is her phone. Sally picks up her phone and answers it. ***Sally's Phone***

STAGE 1 • 400 HEADWORDS

... past simple – coordination with *and*, *but*, *or* –
subordination with *before*, *after*, *when*, *because*, *so* ...

I knew him in Persia. He was a famous builder and I worked with him there. For a time I was his friend, but not for long. When he came to Paris, I came after him – I wanted to watch him. He was a very clever, very dangerous man. ***The Phantom of the Opera***

STAGE 2 • 700 HEADWORDS

... present perfect – *will* (future) – *(don't) have to, must not, could* –
comparison of adjectives – simple *if* clauses – past continuous –
tag questions – *ask/tell* + infinitive ...

While I was writing these words in my diary, I decided what to do. I must try to escape. I shall try to get down the wall outside. The window is high above the ground, but I have to try. I shall take some of the gold with me – if I escape, perhaps it will be helpful later. ***Dracula***

... should, may – present perfect continuous – *used to* – past perfect
– causative – relative clauses – indirect statements ...

Of course, it was most important that no one should see
Colin, Mary, or Dickon entering the secret garden. So Colin
gave orders to the gardeners that they must all keep away
from that part of the garden in future. *The Secret Garden*

... past perfect continuous – passive (simple forms) –
would conditional clauses – indirect questions –
relatives with *where/when* – gerunds after prepositions/phrases ...

I was glad. Now Hyde could not show his face to the world
again. If he did, every honest man in London would be proud
to report him to the police. *Dr Jekyll and Mr Hyde*

... future continuous – future perfect –
passive (modals, continuous forms) –
would have conditional clauses – modals + perfect infinitive ...

If he had spoken Estella's name, I would have hit him. I was so
angry with him, and so depressed about my future, that I could
not eat the breakfast. Instead I went straight to the old house.
Great Expectations

... passive (infinitives, gerunds) – advanced modal meanings –
clauses of concession, condition

When I stepped up to the piano, I was confident. It was as if I
knew that the prodigy side of me really did exist. And when I
started to play, I was so caught up in how lovely I looked that
I didn't worry how I would sound. *The Joy Luck Club*

MORE WORLD STORIES FROM BOOKWORMS